The 12-Step PROGRAM

A DIVA's Guide to Surviving a Recession

By Ché LaRhue

Cover by Adorkable Designs

WWW.BROOKLYNPUBLISHINGGROUP.COM

This book is intended as a general guide to the topics discussed, and it does not deliver accounting, personal finance, medical or legal advice. It is not intended, and should not be used, as a substitute for professional advice (medical, legal or otherwise). The author and the publisher disclaim any liability for any damage resulting from the use of the information in this book. Company names, logos, Web sites and trademarks used in the book belong to the companies that own them. There is no attempt to appropriate these names, logos and trademarks, and none should be construed. Also, there is no endorsement, implied or otherwise, of these companies listed in this book. They are listed so that readers can find more information. Finally, company names, phone numbers, addresses and Web sites may have changed since the publication of this book.

To Chad and Kimora:

Because every DIVA should be lucky enough to have one

Contents

Contents

Remember that the answer to surviving this State of DIVA Emergency that we are facing is within reach with these 12 easy steps!

Ready DIVAs?! Let's get started!

Step 1.
Acknowledge the Problem

Where did it go?!... It was just here?

You've just bought some new duds for your yoga class; you're on your way. You arrive to the class and it's no longer there. WTF!

Another one?

Are you walking pass store windows expecting to see a reflection of your beautiful self? Yes you DIVA – or maybe a nice blouse? Instead you keep getting the same old sign in your face, 'GOING OUT OF BUSINESS'.

Not the same old.

Instead of your usual response, "I can afford to". Your replying to the question asked to why you just bought those new shoes, "I had to, they said 'EVERYTHING' MUST GO".

Where's everybody?

Are you expecting to walk in a store with all eyes on you? Instead you find that the store is fairly empty.

1

Don't worry DIVAS your not alone. Allow me to introduce myself my name is Ché LaRhue and I'm a self-proclaimed DIVA and oh yeah I'm absolutely addicted to the finer things in life. No, I'm not a shopaholic I can restrain myself. I just have very expensive taste in everything from what I wear to what I eat. There I've said it. And if you can admit that you may need help too. So DIVAS I am asking that you put the DIVATUDE to the side and listen up. Sh*t isn't looking to good for us. Were in an extreme State of DIVA Emergency. I don't know about you, so I'll speak for myself - I want what I want when I want it. Now I really can't say that I'm weak just because I love Louis Vuitton, Prada and Gucci can I? Yes I know ... I know. These are pretty expensive brand names I'm throwing out there. And with this being said - this is the problem. Lately I have had to curve my shopping. That means not getting the things that I actually want. With the way things have been going I have had to budget a little more just to have the extras. So with this new me I have had to adjust my

DIVA like behavior when it comes to shopping and what I will be willing to do when it comes to my clothes. After all, it's all in the swag baby. What you wear says a lot about you. Yeah they say it matters what's in the inside, but they pay attention to what's on the outside. Yes there a few out there that would say I'm vain, but what do they know the ones saying that are the ones who sit back silently watching your every move; waiting for you to no longer be able to afford the life that you have become accustomed to. But they can't help themselves and neither can I - I love fashion and as far as I can remember I always have. I love the feeling of stepping in a pair of new Prada shoes or the looks I get when I am walking down the street with my limited edition Red Fendi bag. (FYI – I still have yet to see another soul with it.) I can't remember the last time I put my feet in a pair of shoes that weren't $300 or more. If you're a designer label freak such as myself then you must be having a hard time dealing with the economic crisis just as I am. And if you're anything like me you're finding it quite difficult to cut down on your expenses. People often tell me to cut back on my spending. And I have tried. I try to stay away from designer stores. But what do you do if all you've known is European designers and Domestic Fashionistas? I have such a thing for fashion, its not even funny. I can remember times saying "not this week, not today I will not get those shoes." Than I walk pass a Bergdorf window and see the shoes; I start to catch a sweat, I feel dizzy, all of a sudden very dizzy. Next thing I know I am asking the sales guy to bring me a size 9. There are only a few things that come to mind when I see something that interest me. First, I think about how it would look on me. Second, I look at the price and say to myself that's not so bad – if I don't get this and spend less on that. Just to say the least, whatever the price was I would work out a way to get it. It never occurred to me that I had a problem. Until my salary was cut 20% this is when I knew I had a problem on my hands. I have done some things that I am not proud of for the sake of fashion. And I have come to the point where I think I might need some help. Sooooo, uh – yes I'm addicted to Marc Jacobs and etc; etc…. Whateve's….

Part of the recovery process for me is taking responsibility and no longer using the excuses I once did.

Some of the excuses us DIVAS commonly use for paying too much for clothes and accessories.

Excuse 1: I have expensive taste

Excuse 2: I'm a funny shape

Excuse 3: I had a deprived childhood

Excuse 4: I can afford to

Does any of this sound familiar? I know you don't want to admit it, but DIVA you got it bad.

Answer this short list of questions to see how bad you've got it:

1. Do you have more pairs of shoes in your closet than you could possibly wear in a year?
2. Do you find that you shop at Bloomingdales more than you go grocery shopping?
3. Have you bought a piece of clothing knowing that it was completely unappealing but figured you'd be the one to rock the hell out of it?
4. When meeting someone new, do you associate him or her with the brand of clothing they wore?
5. Are you never the one to miss out on the latest trends of the season?
6. Do you justify new purchases as gifts to yourself?
7. Do you have clothes in your closet with the tags still on them?

Yep, just as I suspected if you have answered yes to any of these questions – its time to move on to step 2.

Step 2.
Think Long Term

Now that you have established that there is a problem we must think about our future and the State of DIVA Emergency we are now facing. Breathe...now is not the time to panic grab a bottle of Smart Water – take a sip, get a pen and now lets think about our future (please see page 19)*. Our clothes must last even if the stores we bought them at don't. Open your closet its time to clean house. Now this doesn't mean throw everything out of your closet and start new. In order to think clearly we need to know exactly what we possess. I advise you to do this when all your clothes are clean and are back from the cleaners. This way you have a clear idea of what you have in your closet. First, we will start out with the clothes that don't fit. The ones you know, that you have and hope to fit in one day. (Not that you wont. With help from my fitness DVD "The 15 Minute Workout - Look Fit n Fab. The Yoga Way". You'll fit in those jeans in no time - Did I just shamelessly plug my DVD? Nope. DIVA Rule #0982. A DIVA has No Shame in Her Game) Even those pair of bell-bottoms you had since I don't know

8

when. When where bell bottoms hot again? Email me that. Really I want to know. But seriously DIVAS, if an item of clothing just can't fit no matter how many Ben and Jerry pops you cut out - just give it up, it isn't worth it there are other people out there that can benefit from them. They can be passed down to family and friends or even **given to charity.**

Here are a few charities that I know:
<u>Salvation Army</u>

Chances are there is a Salvation Army Family Store near you. At your local Salvation Army Family Store you can find great deals and bargain prices on clothing, furniture, household goods, sporting equipment, books, electronics and much more.

For more information visit **www.salvationarmyusa.org**

<u>Goodwill</u> (Become a lifetime member):
Goodwill Industries is all about people working.
North America's leading nonprofit provider of education, training, and career services for people

9

with disadvantages, such as welfare dependency, homelessness, and lack of education or work experience, as well as those with physical, mental and emotional disabilities.

For More information visit **www.goodwill.org**

Or if there's a charity you have in mind and don't know the name visit: **www.charityguide.org**

*Please note: For tax purposes, you should always keep a list of the clothing you donate.

And if you think the garment is way to valuable and you just can't see yourself giving it away hold on to it for when you may want to swap pieces with a friend. Let your friend know just how valuable it is to you and why you like it so much this will only make it easier to persuade the person when negotiating which we will discuss later in step 6.

Since step 2 is all about thinking long term, we'll discuss how to preserve the clothes that we do have.

Undergarments
Care instructions:
Proper care and cleaning extends the longevity of each piece, keeping you in place much longer.

Jeans
Care instructions:
To avoid shrinking jeans, first wash them in cold water, lightly tumble them on warm in the dryer, and then finish drying by hanging overnight.

DIVA TIP 101

To stretch jeans, first wash them in cold water, lightly tumble them on warm in the dryer, put them on slightly damp and dance around until they stretch to where you want them.

11

Shirts

Care instructions: Turn decorated shirts inside out wash with cold water and hang them up to dry- no fading!

Shoes

Care instructions: A magic eraser works well with white sneakers or shoes with a white sole. If you have a slight scuff a little buffing or some shoe polish should do the trick. (Speaking of trick did you know you could get rid of scuffs on suede shoes with a little brush of a nail filer? Pass this tip on to the next DIVA.) And if you're too much of a DIVA to do these repairs yourself spring for a shoe smith to do the work. It won't be so bad. Not as bad as buying a pair of shoes when you could just as simply touch up the ones you already have.

Coats

Care instructions: The ones that are dry clean only Drop them off at the cleaners and where them accordingly. If you posses a peat coat and every DIVA should have one. Pop those collars ladies! A lint brush to them or some masking tape is the key to keeping them looking new and some dry cleaning sheets and a dryer can be used to keep them fresh during wear.

For coats out of season. All I have to say is vacuum bags and a storage bin. It does wonders for storing bulky coats. (Moth balls and cedar hangers a must)

For the longevity of all your garments please make sure to read the care directions on the tags carefully.

After examining your wardrobe and disposing of needless pieces your wardrobe might look a little sad. Cheer up!! If you need to buy new clothes, I mean if you absolutely must, now is the time (yayyy). But first we will need to go over the 70/30 rule. Yes I know no

DIVA likes rules. But this one you will be sure to want to follow and it will actually benefit you. You should keep in mind that the object of this program is to avoid having to buy items that are not needed and work with what you got for now-that is until things get back to stable ground. 70 percent of your wardrobe should consist of classic, standard pieces that can be thrown on at any time and never go out of style in any season. Whether it may be for work, party or just simply a day when you dress down, and if you're like me then days like that are rare (DIVA Rule # 2056 A DIVA must be able to back up her swag at all times). 30 percent of your wardrobe should consist of flashier pieces. Like a designer handbag or a nice necklace something that would bring any outfit to life – These items will be your splurges. Remember to refer to your flashier items as splurges or a reward as a DIVA shouldn't ever have to buy a gift for herself and it's easier to justify them as a reward after not having gone shopping for say about 30 days. Fix your face I know you can do it. ☺

→**Moving right along.** Let's take a look at the classic pieces that every DIVA should have in their wardrobe:

The Black Bra

Avoid preventable fashion mistakes like polka dot and stripe designs under light color tops-the cousins should speak for themselves no need to advertise.

The Skinny Jean

From day to evening, from Sunday brunches to a girl's night out. You can dress them up with just about anything.

Black Dress Pants

A high-quality pair of dress pants will last you a lifetime! Work, interviews or a night out on the town.

Trench Coat

A good trench goes from spring to light summer, fall to early winter- just work it with different accessories.

Pumps

A little height goes a long way and a good pair of leather pumps complements many outfits.

A Full Skirt

A mid-knee or below-the-knee full skirt is a wardrobe must have. Shorter skirt lengths and higher waist styles outdate easily so for longevity consider avoiding these skirt trends.

All-Purpose Handbag

To tote your daily supplies around town, you'll need an all-purpose handbag. One that makes a statement.

Hater Blockers (Sunglasses)

Nothing says DIVA like a pair of sunglasses to protect your eyes through sunny skies and dirty stares by carrying a pair of sunglasses with you everyday. A good pair of sunglasses should protect against UVA rays.

The Little Black Dress

The occasions that fit a little black dress are endless. For an ageless look, find a basic shape like an A-line or empire waist and use different accessories for each occasion.

White Collar Shirt

A crisp, white dress shirt is a wardrobe must-have to provide a base look for seasonal accessories. Spandex blends woven into the cotton allow extra stretch for more form-fitting styles.

DIVAS we know all to well about last minute plans they can end up costing us more than we bargain for. I can't begin to tell you how many times I have been invited to an event and had nothing to wear. And just by having these simple yet classic pieces a DIVA was good to go.

(**Some Advice:** A DIVA's hair should always be on point - manicure & pedicure all ways. No excuses.)

Next, take a look at a few suggestions on how you can mix match these classics to fit the occasion:

White collar Shirt left unbuttoned with a really good push-up bra (the cousins never disappoint me), and a pair of skinny jeans for a girl's night out. Don't forget the heels. Now let's think about the working DIVA, using the same white-collar shirt with a few more buttons closed, a flair skirt and a pair of flats or heels. Your choice. And *voilà* some excellent ways to make otherwise simple looks more sexy and appealing to fit the occasion.

*If you have found that you are missing a few classic pieces take another sip of water, pick up that pen and make a note of it and set a budget to get the item missing from your wardrobe.

Tear or Cut

Step 3.
A Power Greater Than

The "It" Bag

Yes DIVAS I know we have all been mesmerized by the latest it bag and we won't speak of the cost of them just the stigma behind the craze. I once thought that as long as I had this fashion accessory by my side there was nothing that any one could tell me. I have a designer bag for everyday of the week. And let me tell you the looks that I got when I first started sporting my bags have since then faded. Once a bag has gone out of season the next one is in season and the craze begins all over again. The hype is shortly lived and it is not worth the money for just one season of notoriety. I could just as simply changed my hair color and get the same attention. Now I admit the attention I get is flattering, but is it worth this month's rent or mortgage payment?

21

When IT all began...

"Ten years ago your handbag was just a receptacle for purse and keys. Nowadays it's a fashion statement that says more about you than anything else in your wardrobe. Judy Rumbold casts a quizzical eye over a decade of it-bags and the celebrities who have wielded them

Ten years ago no one made a lot of noise about handbags. They were simply humdrum accessories, along with shoes and jewelry that added the finishing touches to clothes. They were practical, functional and not at all sexy. How things have changed. Due to clever marketing, celebrity endorsement and, it seems, feverish acquisitiveness on a monstrous scale, the world has gone mad for bags. The more the better. One for every outfit. In every color and size and myriad combinations of pulse-quickening studs, tassels, quilting and hardware. Now bags are cult items, must-have accessories for which ordinarily sensible women will submit to all sorts of indignities - interminable waiting-lists, unseemly bidding wars on eBay, hissy fits in department-store handbag departments. All because they saw Sienna Miller carrying it in Heat. Is there a woman alive who isn't infected by it-bag fever? Is there a man alive who has the faintest idea why handbags suddenly cost a month's salary? And it all started a decade ago with one little bag from Fendi...

1998 Fendi Baguette

Being named after a loaf may not sound all that promising on paper, but this is the style widely credited as the original it-bag. Designed by Silvia Venturini Fendi to tuck neatly under the arm like French bread, the early designs featured the double-F logo created by Karl Lagerfeld when he began working for the company in 1962. The hype surrounding the Baguette began after the company held a legendary sample sale in New York in December 1997. The bags had yet to take off, and the company offered them to fashion insiders, including many magazine editors, for the breathtakingly low price of £25 each, or £50 for the fur variety. Shortly afterwards, during the European fashion collections in March 1998, armies of fashion folk turned up flaunting their cut-price Baguettes. They were widely photographed, and an it-bag was born. Now more than 600 versions of the Baguette exist, ranging from a £200 black nylon one to a hand-loomed style costing £6,000"

All the It Bags we have come to love:
Hermès Birkin, named after actress Jane Birkin
Hermès Kelly, named after actress and later Princess of Monaco Grace Kelly
Balenciaga Motorcycle
Balenciaga Muse
Bottega Veneta Knot

Botkier Bianca Satchel

Botkier Trigger

Bulga Butterfly

Caprice Bianca Large Weekender

Chanel 2.55

Chloé Edith

Chloé Paddington

Fendi B

Fendi Spy

Givenchy Nightingale

Dolce and Gabbana Lily

Dior Samurai

Kooba Sienna

Louis Vuitton Speedy

Marc Jacobs Stam, named after model Jessica Stam

Marcela Calvet Fay Dorys in alligator

Prada Fairy Bag

Rebecca Minkoff Morning After Bag

YSL Muse

YSL Downtown

Treesje Asher Grande

The "it" Bag. Yes, these simple yet expensive fashion accessories have gotten to our wallets more than once. While it would be nice of luxury retailers to give a deal every once in a while and hook a DIVA up. It would reduce the status of having an "it" bag. It would hurt the very thing that makes a Louis Vuitton bag a Louis Vuitton bag in the first place. While owning something that most people can't have. The "Status Symbol" that we all have come to love over the years is slowing starting to run its course. While it has been fun having the ability to overspend (when I could) times have definitely changed.

The "it bag" has been such the craze; I admit no material is worth the kind of money I have spent on them, them as in plural. All they did was take "high quality bags" and stick a name on them, so of course, now these "limited" bags are everywhere and on everyone. From the 20 something year olds who just got there tax return to the old lady with a walker clutching for dear life onto the present her son got her for mother's day. I mean WTF, man. And what about next season? Besides, why spend that kind of money on a bag when the people that you respect will only notice it once.

This day and age, one must not forget the power of the Internet. Now one can have today's "it bag" by renting it for a week, just go on-line & choose the way you want it shipped to you. And there you go. Now you have the "it bag of the week, season or whatever you're having a taste for, then return it & get the next "it bag". Impress all of your haters and the passerby's on the street.

For more info on where to get the latest "it" bag just flip the script → → →

Borrow or Rent the Latest Authentic Designer Handbags, Purses, Sunglasses, Jewelry, Watches, and Accessories at BagBorroworSteal.com.

It as easy as 1..2...3

1 borrow

Browse for a handbag, jewelry, and sunglasses or watch (or all four!) that you love, and then click "Borrow".

2 enjoy

Keep it as long as you wish. A week! A month!

3 return

Change your look as often as you want. Returns are easy and return shipping is FREE!

Step 4.
Avoid Temptation

"Window shopping" is another one of those things that we DIVAS know all too well - Maybe your passing time between meetings, waiting for a friend or just simply strolling to your next destination allowing the world to get a glimpse of a DIVA in all her GLORY. If there's one thing for certain that I do know is that when we finally decide to enter a store and grace it with our presence - we may have entered with no plans on buying anything. But it doesn't take a rocket scientist to know what happens next.

"**Do you take American Express**?"– Sounds familiar. Sure it does.

Step 4 is not to deter you from window-shopping. Just to give some tips on how to do it. Window-shopping is not like regular shopping where you have an objective (something in mind you want) where you're less likely to stray from it. Window-shopping is a totally different ball game. Often at times when I go out window shopping I end up with things that I had absolutely no intentions on buying. I have items that I bought just because they were on sale and I have never worn them before. I have even gone, as so far to buy things that weren't my size I know that they're not going to fit me. But the price was too good to pass up. Somehow I convince myself that I'm going to drop the weight. It doesn't ever happen that way. In the end the only thing I've done is create a reason to be unhappy and pissed off every time I open my closet. I am constantly reminded of the weight I have gained and have yet to loose. Than I eat something to make myself feel better. I know-what a total contradiction. But if clothes don't do the trick chocolate will. LOL!!

I loved this post that I saw online about a "DIVA" going out window shopping. Check it out:

True story:

"Broke as I am I went window-shopping yesterday. All the stores are at the streets around my apartment at Madison Avenue. Even though it hurts a

little looking at everything I can't afford, it satisfies my need to have constant control of what is in the stores at the moment."

-DIVA Unknown

Oh DIVA! The only control you should be worried about having is over your checkbook.

Tips & Warnings (DIVAS Beware)

Invite a friend or two to window shop with you. Window-shopping is much more fun if you have someone with you. Set a date and time and stick to it. If things don't go as planned agree to another date (try to fight the urge to go by yourself a voice of reasoning is needed when you window shop after all you're a DIVA and sometimes you need a stern talking too). When meeting up get ready for some good gossip while window-shopping. After all you have to make up for lost time. Did you see what whatsaface had on, on "**American Idol**"? Uggh.

If window-shopping by yourself try your local mall. Malls are usually a good place to start. They have department stores that have everything from jewelry to furniture. And who knows you may run into someone to join in on the fun.

Leave your money, credit cards and checkbook at home. Only bring enough MONEY for lunch, if you're planning on making a day out of window-shopping. Otherwise, you might be tempted to purchase something when the purpose of the trip is just to **look**.

Go ahead your going to do it anyway. If you walk pass a store and see something in the window or simply just want to go in and see what's new. Why not?! Just keep in mind your just looking!! There's no shame in "**only looking**". You see something you like try it on - just because you try it on doesn't mean you have to buy it. After all half the fun in window-shopping is trying on clothes so go ahead and enjoy yourself. And by the way the other half is getting a rush just by having it on especially if it's a dress from Marc Jacobs new spring collection. (**Wink**) (**Wink**)

And last but not least. Remember just to enjoy yourself go with the flow and have a good time. And don't think about what the sales assistant thinks or the girl in the fitting room who was standing at the door when you walked in with 6 items and are putting back six items. So what they have to put it back this is their job after all with how the stores are closing down left and right they should be happy to have a job. So in the long run you're helping the economy. In the end window-shopping is relaxing and a great way to spend a day. Just try not to hurt any one while doing it! (that goes for all the Naomi's out there – we don't want to hear about your little window shopping excursion on page 6)

And oh yeah DIVAS I can't stress this enough your just looking – there's no need to spend any money doing it!   *Capisce*!

Step 5.
It' So Hard to Say Good-Bye

So WE won't! Why should WE!

Listen up DIVAS!

For all of you that open an account whenever you're out shopping or hear the question:

"Would you like to save 15% off your purchase today?"

You should be paying extra special attention. Yes, for some the next step would be to say good-bye to our department store credit cards – but that's absolute bullsh*t. And a move for shall I say, L-O-O-S-E-R-S. Imagine that, I say goodbye to Neiman, Bergdorf and my good old friend Mr. Bloomingdales. Ha! That's me laughing. After all they haven't done anything wrong to me. It all lies in the attitude and were working on that as we speak. Now we won't be saying goodbye but we could stand for a break. Not a break-up, just a little time apart. I know... I know what B.S. But this isn't a permanent adios, it's just until were at least able to catch up on all bills and clear up some balances. Having department store credit cards is not necessarily a bad thing. I only use department store credit cards when I can save at least 15% or when it's most beneficial to muah - after all, a DIVA should always ask one self, "What's in it for me". I have a credit card for damn near every department store out there even for ones that are located in a different state different from the one I live in. I try not to leave the house with them. After all a DIVA has to learn how to avoid temptations as per discussed in step 4. A debit card is all I carry especially now in these days.

Now back to the question at hand- who wouldn't want to save 15% in this day and age? But considering the catch to actually get the discount, you have to sign up for the store's credit card. What a surprise. This is a big NO, NO. Why set yourself up for debt. If you can't buy it cash or pay for it in full when the bills comes then say no and walk away. Don't take a second look, not even a second thought just walk away. Pay for the item the way you intended too. Then leave while you still have the chance.

Store cards aren't all bad. The plusses, according to CreditCards.com:

· Store cards are easier to qualify for. If you're trying to build credit and have been turned down by a standard card, a store card can get you over the first hurdle of establishing creditworthiness.

· Since major banks service most store cards, they tend to report promptly to credit bureaus. Remember, no one is required to report credit activity to the bureaus, so sometimes the gossip is welcome - particularly if you need someone to brag on your behalf.

· A lost or stolen store credit card is of limited use to a purse-snatcher. Their shopping spree is confined to that store's locations. As with any missing card, report the theft, pronto -- no matter how many Banana Bucks the thief is racking up on your behalf.

Which department store should you choose?

The one's where you shop at the most, sweetie. For me, that would be SAKS, Bloomingdales, and Macy's they all pretty much work the same way. What you're applying for is a revolving line of credit. If it's your first card, you'll probably receive a low credit limit, like I received my first time. That's a good thing, because you don't to want to spend anywhere close to your limit.

Now you know

Every time you fill out an application for credit, the application is noted on your credit report. While applying for a card tends to have a negligible impact (costing a couple of points or so), too many at one time can take your credit rating down a notch or two. Fair to weak.

Interest rates on department store credit cards are often much higher than a Visa or a MasterCard. So pay your bill in full every month and on time!

Read the fine print.

It may look straightforward, but make sure you find out if there are any fees associated with the store card.

Here are the (**4**) key questions you should ask before opening that account:

Is there an over-the-limit fee?

What is the interest rate?

Is there an annual fee?

What are the late charges?

The Top 10 Department Credit Cards a DIVA Should Have:

1. **Saks Fifth Avenue World Elite MasterCard** - Saks credit card can be used anywhere MasterCard is accepted, and it earns points on all purchases, including up to 6 points per dollar on purchases at Saks Fifth Avenue stores. (www.saksfifthavenue.com)
2. **Macy's Credit Card** - Offers store credit cards with varying Star Rewards levels. (www.macys.com)
3. **Nordstrom Credit Cards** - Offers both Nordstrom-only charge cards and Visa cards with reward points. (about.nordstrom.com)
4. **Neiman Marcus Credit Card** - Well-known department store offers In Circle Rewards for users of its credit card. (www.neimanmarcus.com)
5. **Bergdorf Goodman Credit Card** - Apply here for a credit card from this high-end department store chain, and earn In Circle reward points. (www.bergdorfgoodman.com)

6. **Bloomingdale's Credit Cards** - Credit cards from Bloomie's. (www.bloomingdales.com)
7. **Barneys New York Credit Card** - Store credit card offers reward points. (www.barneys.com)
8. **Lord & Taylor Credit Card** - Offers a credit card for use only at Lord & Taylor department stores. (www.onlinecreditcenter2.com)
9. **Century 21 Department Stores MasterCard** - Credit card can be used anywhere and earns Century 21 reward points. (www.c21stores.com)
10. **Dillard's Credit Cards** - Choose between a Dillard's credit card for use in the department store only, or a Dillard's American Express card that can be used anywhere. Both cards offer reward points. (www.onlinecreditcenter2.com)

For more information on department store credit cards visit:

www.creditcards.com

Remember DIVAS; credit is fine (when not abused). Discounts are great (provided they're for something you were going to buy anyways).

Step 6.
There's Always Room to Negotiate

First we'll start off with a little story:

"I wanted a pocketbook at a well-known high fashion store. It was on display and the last one they had in the store. There were fingerprints all over it, the leather looked obviously worn, after all the hands and try-on's it was not worth the same price. But I had to have it. The sales person wanted to make me feel bad. But f*ck you where's your manager. Story short - I saved 100 bucks on it"

DIVA Anonymous

Did you know:

The pricing technique used by most retailers is cost-plus pricing. This involves adding a markup amount (or percentage) to the retailers cost. Another common technique is manufacturers suggested list pricing. This simply involves charging the amount suggested by the manufacturer and usually printed on the product by the manufacturer.

Rule Number One - Know what you want and how much you're willing to pay for it. Let us say, for example, that you want to negotiate with a sales person on a price for an item at a department store. Like I did – I mean DIVA unknown did. If the item is priced way too high and you find that price to be too F*cking ridiculous - your next step is to negotiate it. First, you will have to figure out how much you think that item is really worth. Let us say that the item in question is $100. Now, decide on a lower price that you can try for, uh... let's say 50 bucks. That's half the original price that's being asked, but it's a good place to start. Finally, decide on the highest price that you will pay for the item, and let us say you will pay no more than $80. Now, offer the seller 50 bucks. He or she might laugh in your face, but hold back all DIVATUDE. If they just won't budge and they're serious about this $100, then you will need some bargaining power on your side. Point out any flaws that you can find on the item. This is a great way to get people to lower their prices. By pointing out any

45

flaws, which make the item seem like it is less valuable than they think it is. You might not care about missing buttons or scratches, but if you get the item for the right price, then you cannot let them know that. And if theirs more of that item in the store forget about negotiating. Its pointless believe me.

Most every day we Divas have a chance to negotiate one if not many types of deals in our lives. Many times DIVATUDE gets in the way - park it. Stay cool. In order to be successful negotiators, we have to know the basics of the game.

Here are a few tactics to negotiate discounts on everything from jewelry to online purchases according to Realsimple.com

Online Purchases
Consider this: You can't haggle online. But there are Websites (such as www.shopzilla.com,

www.froogle.com, and www.nextag.com that track and compare Internet prices for products and direct you to the best bargains. They also rate the sellers based on customer reviews.

Try this: To squeeze the price even further, call a regular store that stocks the product and ask that store to match the best price you saw advertised online. "We are very likely going to drop our price to beat another reputable dealer," says Abe Brown of J&R Music and Computer World. (You can find a list of authorized dealers by contacting the product's manufacturer or, in many cases, just going to its Web site.)

Jewelry

Consider this: The standard selling price for jewelry is 2.3 times the wholesale price, according to the Jewelry Information Center, a trade association. In other words, if the price tag says $500, the jeweler probably paid about $217 for it.

Try this: "Don't just say, 'What's the best price you can give me?'" says jeweler Philip Weisner. "Say, 'Oh, that's more than I am looking to spend.' Then tell him what your budget is. The jeweler may be able to give you the piece you want for your number or direct you to a similar piece you want that's in your price range." Finally, offer to pay with a check. The jeweler may agree to pass along the percentage he would otherwise have been charged by a credit-card company for the transaction.

Chain-store items

Consider this: The salesclerks at chain stores generally don't have the authority to give you a discount, but a manager does.

Try this: If you're buying a big-ticket item ($200 or more), ask managers for a discount, says Eugene Fram, a marketing professor. If you've seen the item in the store for a while, say so. Some stores have codes on price tags that will show the manager how long the product has been on the floor. "The longer it has been hanging around, the better the deal you can get," says Fram. For smaller purchases, ask a clerk if she knows when the item is likely to go on sale, or ask her to call you when it is marked down. You could also tell the cashier you forgot the coupon from the weekly circular. He will probably have an extra.

Professional Services

Consider This: Your relationship counts. "If you're a good client -- someone who has referred other customers, who brings organized documents, who pays bills quickly -- I'll knock 10 percent off my fee if you ask," says accountant Marc Albaum.

Try this: Ask for a loyalty discount. If you're not a longtime customer, go to an accountant or an attorney who does work for your friends or family and ask to receive the same treatment as they do, including any price breaks. Offer a barter payment (designing a new Web site for the firm, say), which benefits her by reducing her taxable income. Or propose that she do the work when it's best for her schedule -- preparing taxes in February, for example -- in return for a lower fee. **Real Simple: Spend money to save money**

Discounts on health and beauty services

Consider this: If you make your appointment for one of the salons slow days, you may be able to negotiate a 10 to 20 percent discount. Referring new customers could also earn you a price break.

Try this: Ask whether you can get a discount for booking on a Monday or a Tuesday, which are often the slow days. Mention any new clients you have steered their way and see if you can broker something in return. You may also get a discount if you buy packages of services. The same strategies work for facials, waxing, and other beauty services, as well as private training sessions, says personal trainer Linda LaRue. "If you pay up front for 10 or 12 sessions or can train during off-hours, I'll knock my fee down by 10 percent," she says.

Mom-and-Pop Stores

Consider this: Whenever you're buying from the owner -- or someone with direct access to the owner -- discounts are easier to get than in chain stores. "The boss has the power to make decisions, he knows his bottom line, and he knows the value of making a sale and establishing good rapport with a customer," says Fram.

Try this: Explain to the store's owner that you're a local customer (if you are) and that you like shopping at independent retailers and coming back to a merchant you know. Mention what the big-box stores are charging for the same item and ask the independent retailer if he will match the price -- or at least come close. If the owner can't budge on price, ask for free delivery for bigger items.

Cell phone(s)/ Service

Consider this: Your opportunity to haggle over cell-phone minutes and features isn't when you're signing up for a new plan. "You'll start getting sales calls a

51

couple of months before your contract runs out, but don't bite," says telecommunications attorney Art Neill.

Try this: Wait until your contract is about to run out, then calls the company's customer-service department. "Their job is to keep you in the fold, and they'll probably throw some extras your way to do it," says Neill. Tell them exactly what you want in terms of a new phone, minutes, and features, based on research you've done about what other companies are offering, and they may stretch the rules to get you to renew. It's always worth talking to a supervisor if others can't help.

And there you go DIVAS some tips on how to negotiate. For more tips visit **www.realsimple.com**

Just remember the object of negotiating is to get what we want without paying a lot for it. Just remember now that we have some helpful tips we can survive this DIVA State of Emergency and we will. Just know that negotiations may not always work out they way we would like so please refrain from pulling out that can of whoop ass. Either pay full price for the item or put it down and walk fiercely away like a true Diva. You didn't need that sh*t anyway.

Step 7.
More Thrift Less Swift

If you're a true DIVA than more than likely you rarely turn down an invitation. But are you always prepared? You shouldn't always have to go out and buy something whenever there is an occasion. Shopping at the last minute doesn't give you enough time to shop around for deals. It's a good idea to have a few classic pieces in the closet. These are items that will never go out of style and the items that were mentioned in Step 2 ← ← Please refer.

Having a few classics on the sideline would save you money in the long run. Instead of having to buy whole outfits. Now if you just have to get a new outfit just do so in advance.

Restrain from this type of behavior. (Please)

For us DIVAS that go though great lengths to get what we want. If it's not using your cell phone to physically get your point across. Or speaking loud on our cell phone while waiting in long lines - to piss off the cashier so they could hurry the F*ck up... we have ways of getting what we want. Even if we have to pay a little bit extra to get it. If a DIVA doesn't get what she wants - well let's just say... all hell breaks out. Not that this type of behavior can't help us. It just can't help us right now. And its not like I agree with this DIVA like behavior but it is what it is. You just can't teach a DIVA new tricks. Step 7 is especially for those DIVAS that like to shop at the last minute - we need something we go out and buy it. Even if while doing so it harms those around us. Patience is a virtue DIVA especially when it comes to shopping I mean just look at the people who shop for hours looking for a bargain in the sales rack. Sure there's times when I ask myself who has time for that. And the answer in the end is the one who comes out saving – that's who.

Finding bargains.

Sales are usually done towards the end of the season when stores are already getting rid of old stuff to make space for the new season. It is better to shop during sales so that you will have more for your money. Check your local newspapers for discount coupons that can be used when shopping. You can also make a trip to the nearest outlet stores that have branded items at 30-70% off the normal prices.

Make a budget and stick to it.

If you are planning a shopping trip in the future, you should be able to make a list of the things that you really need and set a budget. The most important thing in planning ahead is to stick to your plan and budget. Even if you are on a budget, the quality of the clothing is very important, so check if the materials used are of high quality and the clothing is not damaged. Don't get swayed to buying something because it is on sale. Think first if you really need it before you buy it.

Go vintage.

Vintage shopping is not only in right now, but also very cheap. You can go to garage sales, thrift stores and flea markets to find vintage clothing. Although, you need to be careful and inspect the things you want to buy before you purchase them.

Sticking to the One-In-One-Out Rule: Maybe you've made your own resolution to keep a clean, organized home this year. Thrift store shopping makes it very easy to adhere to the one-in-one-out rule. Just donate something old before you pick up something new.

Shop Online

Shops online also have lots of bargains and freebies like free shipping and price discounts. I've listed a few that I just absolutely love they help me to keep my sexy tight and I can do so without spending a ton of mullah. Check them out. And oh yeah tell them the DIVA sent you. Now I don't know if that I'll help you out much I have quite a reputation for being a B*tch.

I don't know why, I am such a sweetie just don't get on my bad side and respect my COUPON code. You guys know who I'm talking too. No names needed.

Shopittome.com - Gilt Groupe – For Divas only. You have to be invited.

asos.com/red - For up to 70% off designer brands

* brandalley.co.uk - Brand Alley is a members-only site that gives you access to private sales of designer brands at very attractive prices (up to 70% off)

Hautelook.com - The sales—which last between 36 and 72 hours—designers include Chanel and Foley+Corinna

Bluefly.com - The sales—which last between 36 and 72 hours—change daily and the designers vary from those you know (Chanel, Foley+Corinna, Seven for all Mankind jeans) to those that are less familiar (like today's sale on Falls)

Badjoan.com - If small, up-and-coming Indie labels are your thing, you must head over to badjoan.com. The site sells sample and overstock items from an array of lesser known designers—all at 80 percent off retail prices

Thesiteguide.com - Internet shopping guru Patricia Davidson guides you through all the sites for women's fashion and accessories. You can look for anything from the little black dress to designer handbags and click straight through to retailers' websites. Her reviews are spot on: this is the place to find well-priced clothes from companies like Joe Browns, Mango and Uniqlo.

Shopping Online is convenient and fast. When a Diva doesn't feel like the mall or wasting time and energy hitting the pavement. These sites are definitely the way to go. Trust.

Step 8.
Say a Prayer

The Diva's Prayer

Armani

Which art in Neiman's

Hallowed be thy shoes

Thy Prada come

Thy Shopping done

On Rodeo

As it is in Paris

Give us this day our Visa Gold

And forgive us our balance

As we forgive those who charge us interest

And lead us not into Penny's

And deliver us from Sears

For thine are the Chanel, the Gaultier and the Versace

For Dolce and Gabbana

AMEX

As if you haven't been saddened by the fact that our country is falling apart before our very eyes so are some of our favorite stores; no matter how much we hear about it in the news or read about it in the paper we are reminded of the recession every time we see a "Going out of Business" sign or another store boarded up on 7th Avenue - it's just F*cking depressing. Although some of them have relocated to that digital home we call the internet. Some of our favorite stores are about to uh DIVAS I dread the words and I know us DIVAS will try our hardest to not file it shall I say chapter 11. OMG that means the store you shopped at last week may not be around next month. If you have been putting off getting something that you know you always wanted you may have to hurry and get to the store and scoop it up and pray that you're happy with it because what you bought today you may not be able to return tomorrow. If you have any gift, money cards or credit slips from these stores mentioned below, make sure you use them, or you may loose the opportunity to! And if you are shopping in a store that you know is about to go out of business you must understand that final sale means **FINAL SALE**. Do not go to the store and shout out obscenities and start throwing things around you will go to JAIL. Please refrain from exhibiting any DIVA like behaviors avoid all problems. Pay careful attention to the signs posted around you. And read your receipt.

Heads up and attention DIVAS

Here are the stores that informed the Security Exchange of their closing plans between October 2008 and January 2009.

Circuit City stores

Ann Taylor- 117 stores nationwide are to be shuttered

Lane Bryant,, Fashion Bug ,and Catherine's to close 150 store nationwide

Eddie Bauer to close stores 27 stores and more after January

Cache will close all stores

Talbot's closing down all stores

J. Jill closing all stores

GAP closing 85 stores

Footlocker closing 140 stores more to close after January

Wickes Furniture closing down

Levitz closing down remaining stores

Bombay closing remaining stores

Zale's closing down 82 stores and 105 after January

Whitehall closing all stores

Piercing Pagoda closing all stores

Disney closing 98 stores and will close more after January.

Home Depot closing 15 stores 1 in NJ (New Brunswick)

Macys to close 9 stores after January

Linens and Things closing all stores

Movie Galley Closing all stores

Pacific Sunware closing stores

Pep Boys Closing 33 stores

Sprint/ Nextel closing 133 stores

JC Penney closing a number of stores after January

Ethan Allen closing down 12 stores.

Wilson Leather closing down all stores

Sharper Image closing down all stores

Loews to close down some stores

Dillard's to close some stores.

Our favorite stores will continue to close if we do not go out there and do what we do best. Now I'm not telling you to go spend your entire trust fund in the Gap but shop responsibly. Buy the things you need. We shouldn't be afraid to go out and continue the things we've been doing. After all were DIVAS we must do our part. If there's any one who can save us. It's us!

Step 9.
Carry the Message to Others

I know DIVAS we can be selfish at times but now is not that time. Pass along that one-day shopping pass if you are done with it. If you know of a sale we want to know too. Helping out the next DIVA is what it's all about and at a time like this everyone could use a deal or two. When I shop I always ask the sales rep that's helping me if they have a card. I do this because I want to keep up with all the sales. And there are times when a sales rep may be reluctant on telling you this information. So the key is building a relationship. Don't just make your purchase and leave the store. Start a conversation with the cashier or the sales person helping you. I can't tell you how many times I've gotten the insider tip on sales. I even have exchanged numbers with a few and even if I had no intention on shopping if the sale sounds to good to pass up. I'm there. Buy a nice little card, depending on how good the tip was and give it to that special sales rep in your life... Go ahead and treat the tipster to something nice. Now don't go overboard. But do look out. After all they will probably receive incentives for making a sale so remember that when there volunteering info. Yes it's nice but what's there motivation. If you receive coupons by email and best believe if you made a purchase on a website and had to enter your email address to register you are receiving all kinds of coupons and notices. Forward these emails to friends - pass along the info. Go ahead its okay to be a nice DIVA! Every once in a while.

These are a few of my favorite sites to browse for unbelievably cheap designer stuff. Usually when you register you'll get email alerts letting you know when new things arrive.

Dailycandy.com

DailyCandy is a free daily e-mail from the front lines of fashion, food, and fun. Sign up to get the scoop on hot new restaurants, designers, secret nooks, and charming diversions in your city and beyond.

The best part is sign up it's free

CatwalkToCloset.com

Cat Walk to Closet is an on-line designer sample sale offering the most wanted international runway collections at sample sale prices. Be the first to know when new stock hits the website by registering.

Ruelala.com

Rue La La is... an exclusive, invitation-only online destination where Members discover premier-brand, private sale Boutiques, each open for just a brief window of time. Our focus is a well-edited collection of sought-after offerings from the best brand names in the world - combined with helpful service.

Billiondollarbabes.com

Billion Dollar Babes, a cutting-edge fashion club that's been around since 2001. They serve up top designers on a silver platter to a lucky few – at ridiculously discounted prices - Yeah; the secret is spreading... fast. It could because of people like me. HeHeHe! That's me laughing ☺

Step 10.
What to Do When You Relapse

I was surfing through the net and stumbled upon this little post/confession:

Confessions of A DIVA who relapsed:

"I purchased about $150 of clothes from a store on Saturday. When I checked my email on Monday I realized that a car insurance premium I had not been expecting was due, and I needed to pay it. So I decided to return the dresses in order to have money to pay it. Priorities stink. They still had the tags on, and I had the original bag and receipt.

I took them back to the store at lunch today and explained to the cashier I needed to return the dresses; they had not been worn, and still had the tags and original receipt. This store's policy is to refund money as long as they original receipt is present and are still tagged, even sale items.

The cashier got snippy and asked WHY I was returning them. I told her my monthly budget didn't justify it

73

(not that it was her business). She said, "Well, you could afford them on Saturday when you bought them, what   changed?"

Whaaaaat? I gritted my teeth and said "Buyer's remorse. Can you credit back my credit card?" She sighed and was all "Hmmpft, ok. Do you know that returned sales hurts the commission of the employee who assisted you?" I gave a non-committal shrug, but inside I was like "I don't care, gimme my money back!"

I loooooove this store, shop there often, it makes up most of my business wear. This is the first time I have ever returned clothes and did not expect to be subject to the inquisition. I have spent several thousand dollars in their store over the last 3-4 years, and this is   a   nationwide   chain.

Was she over the line or should I blow this off? Should I have asked for the manager? I remember the cashier's name and I'm still pretty ill over how she acted towards me, so I'm considering calling the store to tomorrow and complaining"

-DIVA unknown

DIVA unknown you are not alone.

What do you think? Talk to me express your thoughts on this issue or any issue for that matter. And remember:

"A DIVA is a friend in deed,
When a DIVA is their for the next DIVA in need"

Email me at: askchelarhue@gmail.com or chat with me at www.livewithchelarhue.com

If you absolutely can't fight the impulse, just make sure that you buy something from the sales rack! And remember you must share your personal space with others who are rumbling through trying to find the same bargains. So DIVAS please have some patience- put all DIVATUDE in a BOX and leave it with security.

Step 11.
It Works if You Work It

Wow step 11 already? Were almost there. This step is simply appreciating what you got and making the most with it. While you may be asking what you got, that's a question you have to answer. Here are a few questions that I do have answers to:

Question: What "knowing your body" means?

The difference between you wearing a dress from H&M and someone else is your overall swag and the confidence that one displays. Yes DIVAS no one knows quite how to work it like we do. But just remember your body is unique and what might look good on one person may not look good on you. Knowing what makes those special qualities stand out from the rest depends on how well you know your body. And knowing what to put on your body. So what you can't afford that new dress you saw in SAKS you can afford the one you saw at Daffy's and guess what it should look just as good on you when you try it on.

Answer: You have to know and understand what type of body you have and what looks good on it and what does not. Just because you see someone with a dress you like doesn't mean to go out and buy it. Consider what stands out about it and what will it stand out on you. Less take for instance the photos we see in the magazines when two celebrities wore the same outfit and the question is being asked, "Who were it best?"
It's because each garment is going to have a different effect on how it looks and fits on an individual- it's all depends on the shape of the body and how one carries oneself (swag), some things look good and then something's just don't look so nice on others.

Question: **How do I determine what my body shape/type is?**
Everyone naturally has a body type or shape -- Hourglass, Spoon, Ruler or Cone.

Answer the following questions to determine what your body shape/type is:

- o Do you carry extra weight in your upper and lower body, yet your have a skinny waist?

- o Is there a significant difference between the circumference of your hips and waist?

- o Does your boobies stand out just as much as your booty?

More than likely, you are an HOURGLASS.

- o Do you carry most of your weight in your lower body?

- o Are you more slender on the top?

- o Do your eyes go directly to the lower half of your body when you look in the mirror?

More than likely, you are a SPOON.

- Are you pretty much built straight up and down with very few curves?

- Is there little difference in the circumferences of your chest, waist and hips?

More than likely, you are a RULER.

- Do you tend to carry most of your weight in your back, chest, arms and stomach?

- Are you more slender on your lower body?

More than likely, you are a CONE.

Did you know?

Most women are either Spoons or Hourglasses.

Now that I know my shape, what do I do next?

Answer: The next thing you should do is take that list you made earlier (please see step 2) of the things that's missing from your wardrobe. Because DIVAS, its time to start shopping!!! Now is the time to look for those pieces that will extenuate your body shape. Whether you're a Ruler or an Hour Glass work every curve you got. Just be sexy about it. Remember Less is always more. Just because something is revealing doesn't mean it's sexy. Know your body.

Are you walking fiercely down the block to let the world know your coming and you better have my size?

That's what I want to hear DIVAS!

Let me hear you roar!!!

Step 12.
To Shop or Not to Shop

Congratulations! Welcome to the 12th step, DIVAS! Now its time to reflect on what you have learned. You have acknowledged the problem; your thinking more about the bigger picture; you've ordered your first handbag; you've successfully negotiated a lower interest rate on your department store credit card (you go DIVA); Signed up for Dailycandy; called your girlfriend over to go shopping for a black dress or something else off your list and by now you should have definitely finished that bottle of water ... But wait speaking of shopping when should we do that? Is there a perfect time?

The answer is YES.

Knowing when to shop is half the battle. Shopping during holidays is the other half. Buying an outfit at the last minute doesn't allow you to shop around for bargains. True. But when did you go shopping? Try to familiarize yourself with the seasons and the best times to shop. That way you'll save a few bucks and be a step ahead of the rest. And we just love that don't we?!

To make it easier, I found a few tips over at smartmoney.com they spoke to some insiders to uncover when some of the best times to shop are:

Did you know?
Many clothing stores start restocking on Thursday for weekend sales. So it's best to shop on Thurs and Fri evenings.

Clearance sales
When to buy: Jan/February and August/September, when the fashion shows are held and back-to-school bargains are out

Local mall
When to buy: When you go to the mall you will find some of the best bargains for general merchandise on Saturday late afternoons.

Why: because this is when they are clearing stock for the new sales.

Clothing

When to buy: Thursday evenings, six to eight weeks after an item arrives in stores.

Why: After an item lingers in stores a month or more, retailers start dropping its price to get it out the door, says Kathryn Finney, author of "How to Be a Budget Fashionista." These season-end clearances tend to be the same month that designers host fashion weeks (February and September) to preview the next fall or spring collections. So smart buyers can check the catwalk to see if any of this season's trends — say, leggings or military-style jackets — will still be hot next year, and then scoop them up on clearance.

Hitting the mall on a weekday ensures you'll get a good selection. "On the weekend, you'll only get picked-over stuff because the stores don't have time to restock," she says. By Thursday, most of the weekend sales have begun, but everything available is on the floor.

So, you have to buy your winter coat or fall boots during the months of January and February. These are the months when most stores hold sales for their fall and winter clothes. On the other hand, August and September are the best months to buy your summer and spring clothes.

Shopping is a favorite past time for many DIVAS, and it is something that we do all year round. However, shopping for different seasons of the year will dictate what kinds of things we will buy. Then again, buying certain things at a time when they are in high demand may not necessarily be a good idea. Give a trend some time to fade out and then bring it back out on their ass. One word – FIERCE.

<u>Buy clothes during off-season</u>

Basically, purchasing the latest in fashion trends as they are released means that you have to pay more for your clothes. As such, those who wish to save should buy off-season. This means that you have to buy your winter clothes in summer or fall, and your summer clothes during winter.

Well, this about sums it up for us Divas, I hope you took some good notes – It's up to us now. Remember that for others this may be a recession but for us it should be a lesson that we base off other peoples mistakes and we should try our best not to make the same ones. Continue to be the DIVA you are just do so according to the times – we are in a State DIVA of Emergency, and yes while there are many ways to survive this crisis these simple 12 steps helped me.

Good Luck DIVAS!

Ché LaRhue, **xoxo**

The Diva Planner   2009

January	February	March
Su Mo Tu We Th Fr Sa	Su Mo Tu We Th Fr Sa	Su Mo Tu We Th Fr Sa
1 2 3	1 2 3 4 5 6 7	1 2 3 4 5 6 7
4 5 6 7 8 9 10	8 9 10 11 12 13 14	8 9 10 11 12 13 14
11 12 13 14 15 16 17	15 16 17 18 19 20 21	15 16 17 18 19 20 21
18 19 20 21 22 23 24	22 23 24 25 26 27 28	22 23 24 25 26 27 28
25 26 27 28 29 30 31		29 30 31

April	May	June
Su Mo Tu We Th Fr Sa	Su Mo Tu We Th Fr Sa	Su Mo Tu We Th Fr Sa
1 2 3 4	1 2	1 2 3 4 5 6
5 6 7 8 9 10 11	3 4 5 6 7 8 9	7 8 9 10 11 12 13
12 13 14 15 16 17 18	10 11 12 13 14 15 16	14 15 16 17 18 19 20
19 20 21 22 23 24 25	17 18 19 20 21 22 23	21 22 23 24 25 26 27
26 27 28 29 30	24 25 26 27 28 29 30	28 29 30
	31	

Holidays and Observances

Jan 1 New Year's Day

Jan 19 Martin Luther King Day

Feb 14 Valentine's Day

Feb 16 Washington's Birthday

Apr 12 Easter Sunday

May 16 Armed Forces Day

May 25 Memorial Day

Jul 4 'Independence Day'

88

The Diva Planner   2009

July	August	September
Su Mo Tu We Th Fr Sa	Su Mo Tu We Th Fr Sa	Su Mo Tu We Th Fr
1 2 3 4	1	1 2 3 4
5 6 7 8 9 10 11	2 3 4 5 6 7 8	6 7 8 9 10 11
12 13 14 15 16 17 18	9 10 11 12 13 14 15	13 14 15 16 17 18
19 20 21 22 23 24 25	16 17 18 19 20 21 22	21 22 23 24 25 26
26 27 28 29 30 31	23 24 25 26 27 28 29	28 29 30
	30 31	

October	November	December
Su Mo Tu We Th Fr Sa	Su Mo Tu We Th Fr Sa	Su Mo Tu We Th Fr Sa
1 2 3	1 2 3 4 5 6 7	1 2 3 4
4 5 6 7 8 9 10	8 9 10 11 12 13 14	6 7 8 9 10 11
11 12 13 14 15 16 17	15 16 17 18 19 20 21	13 14 15 16 17 18
18 19 20 21 22 23 24	22 23 24 25 26 27 28	21 22 23 24 25 26
25 26 27 28 29 30 31	29 30	28 29 30 31

Holidays and Observances

Sep 7 Labor Day	Nov 26 Thanksgiving Day
Oct 12 Columbus Day	Dec 24 Christmas Eve
Oct 31 Halloween	Dec 25 Christmas Day
Nov 11 Veterans Day	Dec 31 New Years Eve

DIVA Notes

DIVA Notes

DIVA Notes

THE DIVA PAGES

Is there a spot that you go to that no matter the expense you absolutely cannot see yourself without it? Well here are some of my absolute FAV spots in N.Y. that know how to treat a DIVA like a DIVA.

Time Salon

♥ ♥ ♥ ♥ ♥

Category: Hair Salon

Looking to reinvent yourself or just a signature DO-This is the place-Expect to get a compliment as soon as you walk out the door For more information check them out online.

Dashing DIVA

♥ ♥ ♥ ♥ ♥

Category: Nail Salon

A SANITARY, unique, and fun atmosphere where you can relax and unwind with friends. It's more than a nail salon, Dashing DIVA is a destination.

For store locations visit …….....................……….www.dashingDIVA.com

Beacons Closet

♥ ♥ ♥ ♥ ♥

Category: Clothing Exchange Store

Beacon's closet is not a consignment shop. This means that you don't have to wait for your items to sell before you get cash or store credit for them. This is definitely a spot to got to if you're a DIVA a little strapped for cash and are looking to get rid of the clothes you had from like 2 seasons ago. ☻

The only catch is that you have to make it to Brooklyn and out.

Hey a DIVA's GOTTA do what a DIVA's GOTTA do.

For store locations visit…………………………......www.beaconscloset.com

Still looking for a yoga class?

Crunch Gym

♥ ♥ ♥ ♥ ♥

Category: Physical Fitness

Crunch is based in New York City with 28 state-of-the-art gyms in locations such as Los Angeles, San Francisco, Miami, Chicago, Atlanta and, of course, New York.

For locations near you visit……….………………......www.crunch.com

2010 DIVA Day Planner

Based on the best-selling book "The 12-Step Program...The DIVA's Guide to Surviving a Recession" this stylish planner is as beautiful as it is useful. Featuring quotes from Maya Angelou to Niche, it also serves as a daily reminder of the simple, but important things that we DIVAS tend to forget on a regular basis. From everything to your calorie intake to the amount of water you drink daily, the DIVA Day Planner is your solution for staying on top of things and not on top of your assistant. LOL! ☺

Specifications:

All DIVA Day Planners are spiral bound and printed on recycled paper. Each one is made by hand and is unique from the next.

To place your order, simply complete the order form on the next page or visit www.brooklynpublishinggroup.com

Payment MUST be submitted with order

Thank You for Your Continued Support of our Products

Please note a portion from the proceeds is given to charity.

Year 2010 DIVA Day Planner – Order Form

Name:
_____

Address: _____ City: _____

Province/State: _____ Zip Code: _____

E-mail: _____ Tel: _____

*Orders will be adjusted to include sales tax.

Product Name	Price	QTY.	Total Price
DIVA Day Planner	**$9.99**		$_____+$3S/H
PAYMENT: ☐ VISA ☐ MC M.O. accepted No CHECKS			
Card#			EXP Date:
Authorized Signature (as it appears on card)			

Mail to: Brooklyn Publishing Group

PO BOX 555

Radio City Station

New York, New York 10101

Bibliography

No DIVA knows every thing. As much as we think we do. There are times when we have to swallow our pride and ask others for advice. But the trick is not to let them know that this is the case. However I would have never recovered without the help of my wonderful mother Sharon AKA 'Momma Bear', family, friends and the experts that made this book possible. So I would like to extend special thanks to the following:

Crystal Marrero **(My #1 FAN and BFF)**

Priscilla 'Lola Vegas' Bennett **(Diva-Partner in Crime)**

Yanika Jordan **(My Down-Ass Diva)**

Janika Bailey **(My favorite fashion designer)**

Bernadette Perkins **(More than just a co-worker)**

Antonio Jones **(The Man, The Myth my Little Bro)**

Sheldon Harris **(My BIG BRO)**

Professor Jack Taub **(My favorite English teacher)**

Professor Pinto **(My favorite Mental Health teacher)**

Professor Leonard Hebér **(The one and only HEBĒR)**

Craig Seitel **(The Boss)**

http://www.usatoday.com/money/perfi/basics/2008-03-06-shopping-quality-clothing_N.htm

http://www.thebudgetfashionista.com

http://latimesblogs.latimes.com/alltherage/2008/01/the-it-bag-is-d.html

http://www.nytimes.com/2007/11/01/fashion/01BAGS.html

http://www.bagsnob.com/

http://online.wsj.com/public/article_print/SB120130075401617979.html

http://www.bagborroworsteal.com/

http://en.wikipedia.org/wiki/It_Bag

http://fashionista.com/2009/03/the_it-bag_antidote.php

http://www.nbcnewyork.com/around_town/fashion/Bagged__The_concept_of_the__It_bag_____.html

http://en.wikipedia.org/wiki/Shopping

http://www.answerbag.com/articles/How-to-Go-Window-Shopping/3b7b8fb7-df6a-05af-86bf-b300fe2e8cef
http://consumereducation.suite101.com/article.cfm/department_store_credit_cards

http://www.essortment.com/all/howtonegotiate_rjvf.htm

http://www.cnn.com/2008/LIVING/wayoflife/02/13/negotiate.anything/www.Realsimple.com

http://www.smartmoney.com/spending/deals/the-best-time-to-buy-everything-20025/

http://reviews.ebay.com/THE-BEST-TIME-TO-SHOP-TO-GET-THE-BEST-DEALS_W0QQugidZ10000000004500290

http://www.splendicity.com/thelistmaven/10-reasons-its-time-to-buy-a-new-bra/

http://plonkee.com/2008/03/26/my-top-5-excuses-for-paying-too-much-for-clothes/

http://www.3smartcubes.com/pages/tests/bodyshape/bodyshape_questions.asp

www.ingramcontent.com/pod-product-compliance
Lightning Source LLC
Chambersburg PA
CBHW051043030426
42339CB00006B/179